THE NEED TO KNOW LIBRARY™

# EVERYTHING YOU NEED TO KNOW ABOUT MINDFULNESS



KERRY ELIZABETH BENSON

Rosen YA™
New York

*To Magdalyn Fiore, for her friendship, research help, and writerly advice, and to my mother, for her endless love and support*

Published in 2020 by The Rosen Publishing Group, Inc.
29 East 21st Street, New York, NY 10010



First Edition



**Library of Congress Cataloging-in-Publication Data**

Names: Benson, Kerry Elizabeth, author.
Title: Everything you need to know about mindfulness / Kerry Elizabeth Benson.
Description: First Edition. | New York : Rosen Publishing, 2020. | Series: The need to know library | Includes bibliographical references and index.
Identifiers: LCCN 2018045819| ISBN 9781508187554 (library bound) | ISBN 9781508187547 (pbk.)
Subjects: LCSH: Mindfulness (Psychology)
Classification: LCC BF637.M56 .B46 2018 | DDC 158.1/3—dc23
LC record available at https://lccn.loc.gov/2018045819

*Manufactured in the United States of America*

# CONTENTS

# INTRODUCTION

On June 23, 2018, twelve boys and their twenty-five-year-old soccer coach, Ake, parked their bikes at the entrance to an underground cave in Thailand and stepped inside to explore. One of the players, nicknamed "Night," was turning sixteen that day; his teammates had chipped in to buy him a bunch of snacks as a gift. His family was waiting for him to return home so they could celebrate with dinner and cake.

He never arrived. While the team was inside, the cave flooded with heavy rain, trapping them with limited food and a dwindling supply of air. To survive, they relied on dripping water, Night's birthday snacks … and meditation.

Ake had previously trained as a Buddhist monk, and as he and his soccer players waited in total darkness for an uncertain rescue, he taught them meditation techniques to help them manage their stress, preserve their energy, and reduce their oxygen intake.

Experts say that these techniques may have helped save their lives. By the time two British divers discovered the team, nearly ten days had passed—yet all were alive, and all were remarkably calm.

Ake and the boys tapped into an ancient art as they waited in that cave, as meditation techniques have been traced to 2,500-year-old Buddhist traditions. But you don't have to be Buddhist to practice these coping strategies,

A Thai soccer team (shown here) and their coach were rescued from a flooded cave in 2018. The team used meditation techniques to stay calm as they awaited help.

and you don't have to wait until you're trapped in a cave. Anyone can learn them, and hundreds of millions of people have. And one of the most common forms of meditation is mindfulness.

Over the years, the term "mindfulness" has taken on many different meanings. According to *The Mindful Day* author Laurie J. Cameron, "You can be mindful without

People often associate this cross-legged pose with meditation, but you don't have to sit like this to be mindful. Mindfulness can help people of all ages, backgrounds, and beliefs.

The character Ron Weasley is seen here in a scene from *Harry Potter and the Prisoner of Azkaban*. Mindfulness is its own kind of magic: it gives us powerful strategies to help us cope with life's challenges.

spiders, jobs, difficult relationships, or any of the other countless daily stressors that most people face. It isn't even about changing what people think. Instead, it's about becoming more aware of how they're thinking about and sensing the world. Mindfulness is about making a conscious effort to observe the thoughts, emotions, and sensations that enter their bodies and minds and accessing a powerful coping strategy to deal with the challenges of life.

## MINDFUL CELEBRITIES

**Many celebrities have spoken out about the benefits of mindfulness and similar forms of meditation. Here are just a few. These quotes were excerpted from Essex Meditation (www.essexmeditation.org).**

- **Jennifer Aniston, actress best known for her role as Rachel on the TV show *Friends:*** "Twenty minutes, you just notice the difference! When I get lazy and don't get it in, I can feel a difference in the day."
- **Ellen DeGeneres, comedian and television host:** "It feels good. Kind of like when you have to shut your computer down, just sometimes when it goes crazy, you just shut it down and when you turn it on, it's okay again. That's what meditation is to me."
- **Paul McCartney, singer and instrumentalist for the Beatles:** "In moments of madness, meditation has helped me find moments of serenity—and I would like to think that it would help provide young people a quiet haven in a not-so-quiet world."

People from all walks of life practice mindfulness and similar meditation techniques, including celebrities such as comedian and TV host Ellen DeGeneres.

- **Steve Jobs, cofounder of Apple, Inc., and CEO of Apple until his passing in 2011:** "If you just sit and observe, you'll see how restless your mind is. If you try to calm it, it only makes it worse, but over time it does calm, and when it does, there's room to hear more subtle things—that's when your intuition starts to blossom and you start to see things more clearly and be in the present more."

## SKEPTICAL? LET SCIENCE CHANGE YOUR MIND!

Ever hear the expression "It's all in your head?" When people say that, they usually mean something isn't real. Mindfulness is different. Sure, as a form of brain training, mindfulness is "all in your head"—but it's definitely real! However, despite years of research, it has been difficult to pin down its impacts on the body and mind.

Why is it so hard to figure out the science behind mindfulness? For starters, its effects are much harder to quantify than the effects of a pill. It's easy to measure changes in heart rate after someone swallows medication, but it's not so easy to measure the increases in calmness or focus that people often report after mindfulness training. Another challenge? Mindfulness research isn't standardized, which means participants in different studies aren't necessarily practicing the same techniques, and they might be training for different lengths of time. Still, the emerging research has been incredibly promising.

## RESHAPING YOUR BRAIN

With today's technology, scientists can look at pictures of the brain to determine how it changes after mindfulness—and even during mindfulness exercises. They've come forward with some amazing findings. One of those is that brain changes can happen quickly, even after just eight weeks of practice. These changes aren't just in one spot, either. They happen all over the brain.

In particular, mindfulness training has been shown to increase the activation and change the structure of brain areas called the prefrontal cortex and anterior cingulate cortex, which are involved in regulating attention and emotion—so perhaps that's why so many mindful people report improvements in both focus and emotional control. Other studies, cited in the 2015 *Nature Reviews Neuroscience* article "The neuroscience of mindfulness meditation," have suggested that it helps turn on the insula—a brain area responsible for awareness and emotional processing—and turn off the amygdala, a brain area responsible for processing fear. According to science, then, mindfulness can quite literally turn off fearful emotions while turning on focus and emotional control.

## DON'T GO VIRAL: BOOSTING THE IMMUNE RESPONSE

Imagine having to stand in front of a microphone to give a speech to a panel of judges, all while being filmed.

No notes are allowed, and the topic isn't revealed until three minutes before the presentation. Then, perform five minutes of mental math under pressure. Does that sound like more than enough? Then watch as laboratory researchers smear an irritating, blister-forming cream—made from the substance that gives chili peppers their heat—onto your forearm.

These events took place as part of a study published in *Brain, Behavior, and Immunity* in 2012, and perhaps most surprising is that forty-nine people volunteered to participate, all in the name of science. But here's another (fantastic) surprise: the lucky participants who underwent eight weeks of mindfulness training experienced significantly less inflammation from the blister-forming cream compared to those who did not train in mindfulness. What does this result mean? Well, it suggests that the mindfulness-trained participants were able to better cope with the stress of public speaking (and public math), and these healthier coping skills helped their bodies react in a healthier way, too.

Mindfulness could also help prevent colds and flu. In 2013, researchers at the University of Wisconsin found that participants who had practiced eight weeks of mindfulness meditation were significantly less likely to come down with a cold or the flu compared to participants who received eight weeks of moderate exercise training or no training at all. Even if they did get sick, the mindfulness group reported less severe symptoms than did either of the other two groups.

Scientific studies have shown that mindfulness techniques can help people cope with the stress of public speaking and other types of anxiety-provoking situations.

## EASING ANXIETY AND DEPRESSION

Many teenagers turn to mindfulness to cope with anxiety and depression—and for good reason; it's a great way to help with these issues. In fact, an Oxford University study from 2016 suggested that mindfulness may be just as effective as antidepressant medications for some people. In this study, the people who received mindfulness training and stopped using antidepressants were 23 percent less likely to relapse and have another depressive episode compared to those who continued taking antidepressants without practicing mindfulness.

Mindfulness could be a powerful, no-side-effects alternative to medications—but before making that switch, it's important to check with a doctor, psychologist, or other licensed mental health professional. And don't feel pressured to switch at all: studies have shown that mindfulness can also benefit those who practice it in addition to taking antidepressant or antianxiety medications. Even teens without an anxiety disorder or depression often report feeling less anxious and more content in their everyday lives after mindfulness training. The bottom line is that mindfulness can help teens in a variety of situations. Maybe you're currently taking medications for a diagnosed mental health condition, or

Mindfulness techniques can help teens who are dealing with anxiety and depression, as well as those without a diagnosed mental illness, feel happier and less stressed.

perhaps you feel sad and anxious only every now and then. Either way, it's worth giving this technique a try.

There's more to mindfulness than just science. Sure, structural changes in the brain are pretty cool, and who doesn't want a healthier immune system? These goals are often a huge motivator for people who are just beginning to explore mindfulness, and that's fantastic. But as they continue on their journeys, they just might discover an even better reward, one that is much more challenging to measure: a calmer, happier, more compassionate mind.

## THE MINDFULNESS MARATHON: PRACTICE AND "FAILURE"

Like any other skill, mindfulness takes time and practice. One session is a great start, but persistence is key. After all, if a beginner athlete wanted to become a marathon runner, she wouldn't expect to be ready for a race after one day of practice or even after a week or a month's time. But little by little, as she ran every day, her speed would increase and her endurance would improve. Some days would be harder than others, and she'd be tempted to give up, but she'd press on as she envisioned crossing that finish line. When her legs would burn and her muscles ached, she'd welcome the feeling, because it would mean she was building strength. Think of mindfulness in the same way and try the following suggestions:

- **Make time:** Twenty to thirty minutes of mindfulness each day would be ideal, but even a few consistent minutes each day is helpful. Just give it a try. In fact, busy people often report feeling like they have more time after they start tuning into the world because the minutes and hours no longer slip by unnoticed.

Add mindfulness into your schedule wherever it will fit best. Some people prefer to practice it before getting out of bed in the morning, while others prefer setting aside the minutes before they go to sleep at night; there's no "correct" time as long as it's consistent. Mindfulness can also be easily incorporated into daily activities, such as chores, showers, or the walk to school.

- **Try not to worry about "failure":** Sometimes, people feel like they're no good at mindfulness, or they become discouraged because they've been skipping sessions, so they stop. But there's no pressure and no failing in the process of mindfulness. When people notice their thoughts are wandering or they aren't living in the present moment, that's simply an opportunity to notice what's happening and refocus. Celebrate your struggles throughout mindfulness training because improvement comes by noticing those struggles.

Remember, mindfulness involves restructuring and rewiring the brain, and those changes don't happen overnight. Just as athletes and musicians need to practice to improve, so do people who are training in mindfulness—be patient and kind to yourself throughout this process, and keep at it. The rewards are worth it!

# MYTHS AND FACTS

**MYTH:** Mindfulness takes a lot of time.

**FACT:** Mindfulness does not have to take much time at all. For the best results, many instructors recommend dedicating twenty to thirty minutes per day to being mindful, but if that feels like too much, try ten minutes, five, or even two.

**MYTH:** Mindfulness is only for spiritual people.

**FACT:** Mindfulness is for anyone and everyone: atheists and people of faith, guys and girls, skateboarders, dancers, writers, mathematicians, and people who stay up late watching cat videos on YouTube.

**MYTH:** "Living in the present" means I don't have to study for my math test tomorrow.

**FACT:** Although it may be tempting to skip out on that study session, that's not at all what mindfulness is about. Mindful people still reflect on the past and plan for the future, but they learn strategies to help prevent memories and future events from becoming overwhelming. Instead of panicking about that upcoming math test, they can pause and ask themselves, "What do I need to do in this moment to tackle this test?"

# CHAPTER TWO

# PUTTING MINDFULNESS INTO PRACTICE

Becoming mindful is a matter of training your mind, and there are specific exercises that can help anyone do just that!

## A WONDERFUL EXCUSE TO EAT CHOCOLATE

The first assignment on this journey to mindfulness? Eat chocolate. Any chocolate will do, or try this exercise with your favorite food. Remember, this exercise is not a speed-eating contest; imagine you're a professional taste tester. (The following exercise has been adapted from *Mindfulness: An Eight-Week Plan for Finding Peace in a Frantic World*, by Mark Williams and Danny Penman.)

- With the wrapper still on, run your hands over the chocolate bar. Are there any bumps or ridges through the wrapper, or is it smooth?
- Unwrap the chocolate. What does it smell like? Does the scent remind you of anything?

- What does it look like? Are there any words or designs etched into it?
- Nibble off a piece and let it sit on your tongue for a few moments. What flavor or flavors do you notice? Is it sweet? Is there any bitterness? How about textures—creamy, smooth, crunchy, grainy? Does the taste or texture change at all as it melts on your tongue?
- When you're ready, take another bite. This time, pay attention to the sounds as your teeth sink into it. Then, chew slowly, focusing again on textures and flavors.
- When you swallow, notice how it feels when it

You can easily incorporate mindfulness into your daily life by consciously tuning in to your senses when you eat your favorite foods.

slides down your throat. See if you can trace the feeling beyond that as the chocolate moves into your stomach.

- Continue taking small bites until you're finished, taking mental note of as many sensory details as possible: taste, sight, touch, smell, and sound. If your thoughts start to wander, don't worry: just use your senses to gently refocus your mind on the chocolate.

Now take a moment to reflect on this experience, keeping in mind that there are no right or wrong answers. Was it more enjoyable than mindless, rushed eating? Did you feel impatient at all? Did you notice any sensory details you hadn't thought about before?

By now, you've probably guessed that the takeaway from this exercise is bigger than "Chocolate is fantastic" (although that's a true statement!). Ultimately, when people slow down and focus on what they are experiencing, those experiences change, and they notice details that they usually overlook in their day-to-day lives. They can't slow down time or add more hours to the day, but they can use mindfulness to get more out of each moment.

## CHECKING IN: THE BODY SCAN

The body and the mind are incredibly interconnected. Daily stress and worries often trigger a bunch of different physical symptoms, like stomachaches, headaches, sweaty palms, and tense muscles—and in turn, these issues spill over into the mind to create anxious feelings. It's an all-too-familiar vicious cycle for many people, but here's the good news: A calm, relaxed body can help release tension in the mind, so it also works in reverse. The first step to reversing that cycle is to increase body awareness.

Start by setting aside five or ten minutes each day—maybe just after waking or just before going to sleep—to "check in" with your body using this exercise. With practice, it'll get easier and easier, and feel free to change it up. Some people prefer to start by focusing on their stomach, for example. Others start at their feet and work their way up.

As you do this exercise, sometimes it helps to imagine your attention as something visible, like a laser pointer or a spotlight that travels along the body and explores the sensations in each body part.

- Find somewhere comfortable, ideally a quiet place to lie down and be alone. Close your eyes and take a few deep breaths. With each breath, imagine you're breathing in calm feelings and breathing out tension. Then, tune into the feeling of the mattress beneath you (or the carpet, chair, and so forth, if you aren't lying on a bed).
- Start with the scalp and forehead. What sensations do you notice here? If it's hard to pin down a sensation and it doesn't feel like much, that counts: focus on the absence of feeling there. Is your brain buzzing with thoughts? If so, don't try to force them out; just notice them and gently

lead them back to this exercise.

- When you're ready, slide that attention down and focus on each part of the face: eyes, nose, ears, mouth, jaw, chin. See if you can soften the muscles there, letting go of any tension you might be feeling.
- Slowly slide your focus down to the neck, shoulders, and chest. If the shoulders are scrunched and tense, let them relax, pressing them gently into the mattress or chair. Feel the breath in the throat and chest with each inhale and exhale, and focus again on breathing out tension.

Physical tension often leads to anxious thoughts and feelings. The body scan exercise helps release this tension for a calmer, more relaxed body and mind.

- Move your attention to the stomach. Notice how it moves up and down with each breath. If there's any tightness, breathe it out, allowing those muscles to soften.

- Move to the left arm. As it rests to one side, notice any sensations in the upper arm, then the lower arm, hand, and each finger. Allow those muscles to relax even more as you breathe in calm feelings and breathe out tension. Repeat with the right arm.
- Focus on the left thigh, and see if you can feel the muscles there. Notice the surface that supports the leg, and allow yourself to relax further into that surface. Repeat with the right thigh.
- Now pay attention to the left knee, right knee. Left calf, right calf.
- Move to the left foot. Start by paying attention to feelings in the heel, then the arch of the foot, then each toe. Repeat with the right foot.
- Now focus on the body as a whole, imagining each breath relaxing you from head to toe.

With practice, this check-in exercise will begin to feel easier and more natural. You can also adapt this strategy and use it for just a few moments at a time to help regulate your body no matter where you are.

## MINDFUL EXERCISING: NOT AN OXYMORON

Yes, "mindful exercise" might seem contradictory at first, but don't be fooled! A morning run, midafternoon session at the gym, or evening sports practice are fantastic opportunities to improve mindfulness

Athletes and casual exercisers alike often turn to mindfulness to improve their performance and bring more satisfaction to their workouts.

skills and breathe new life into a workout. In fact, renowned meditation expert Jon Kabat-Zinn trained the 1984 US Olympic Men's Rowing Team in mindfulness. If summoning the motivation to get moving is a struggle, here's some encouraging news: a 2016 study from Utrecht University in the Netherlands found that being mindful can make exercise routines more enjoyable. So give these tips a try:

- **Tune in:** Yank those headphones out, close that magazine, and turn off the TV. Instead of trying to tune out your exercise routine, try tuning in this time. What do you see, smell, hear, and feel? Hone in on something specific, like the rhythm of your breathing, the pounding of your feet on the pavement, or a scuff mark on the treadmill belt that keeps sliding back into view. Periodically redirect that focus to a different sensory detail.

- **Notice:** Pay attention to your body and your mind. Acknowledge negative feelings, like self-conscious thoughts or a reluctance to continue, as well as positive feelings—embrace that runner's high! Take note of physical sensations too, like fast breathing, a racing heartbeat, or a burning bicep.
- **Exercise kindness:** Tell yourself you are enough just as you are, and try to appreciate all that your body can do without comparing yourself to the people around you.

## THERE'S AN APP FOR THAT

**A quick internet search will reveal hundreds of mindfulness videos, apps, and podcasts. Technology is by no means a necessity for mindfulness, so don't feel pressured to use it, but many users appreciate the audio guidance, schedules, and other perks that it can offer. Here are just a few popular options:**

- **Insight Timer:** With millions of users, the Insight Timer app offers thousands of free guided meditations led by many different mindfulness experts, and it has some great talks and podcasts, too.
- **Headspace:** Tens of millions of people have downloaded this top-rated app, which contains playful

animations and a variety of conversational guided meditations. The ten-day beginner's package is free, but unlocking more sessions requires a subscription.

- **Calm:** Apple voted this app the 2017 App of the Year. It's similar to Headspace and Stop, Breathe & Think, but with a, well, calmer, less playful feel. This one's also subscription based, but the first several sessions are free.
- **10% Happier with Dan Harris:** A weekly podcast hosted by ABC newsperson Dan Harris, who authored a bestselling book on meditation after experiencing a panic attack live on ***Good Morning America.***

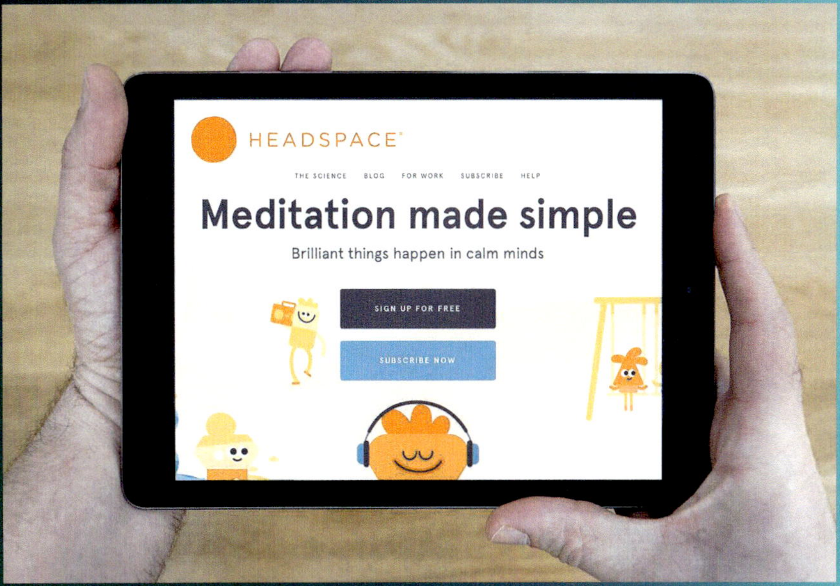


Technology is optional in the world of mindfulness, but many teens find that apps provide helpful guidance and keep them focused and engaged.

## TACKLING ANXIETY AND NEGATIVE THOUGHTS

Anxiety isn't necessarily a bad thing; to a certain extent, worrying helps you anticipate and problem-solve potentially difficult situations before they arise. In fact, some research suggests that highly intelligent people are more likely to be anxious. Still, sometimes a thought emerges—maybe, "I'm so awkward! I can't believe I just said that!"—and a gut-wrenching downward spiral begins. The panicked brain starts reliving every embarrassing-comment, too-loud-sneeze, toilet-paper-stuck-to-shoe moment it has ever experienced. Suddenly, a few seconds of awkwardness grows into something completely overwhelming, and that initial "I'm so awkward" feels like a fact.

But worries aren't necessarily reality; when they arise, label them for what they are. Instead of "I'm going to mess up this presentation," tell yourself, "*I'm having a thought that* I'm going to mess up this presentation." Sure, it may happen—but it may not! Don't give that thought more power than it deserves.

Another helpful strategy is to greet difficult emotions in a friendly way, as if they're visitors just passing through. While it may be tempting to try to ignore or suppress them, avoidance offers only temporary relief. Like a small child demanding attention, it'll keep on prodding and pestering until it's acknowledged. And trying to fix negative thinking often leads to unhelpful self-questioning like, "Why am I feeling this way? Will it ever get better? Why am I such a failure?" Instead, simply labeling feelings without self-judgment can prevent them from building up and becoming overwhelming. So try offering them a moment of casual, cheerful attention: "Aha! There's worry again!" or "That's sadness swinging by for a visit!"

## ALL WHO WANDER ARE NOT LOST

Everybody's thoughts wander. According to a 2007 study by the University of Toronto, the human brain has two separate circuits: the default circuit (also known as the narrative/story circuit) and the direct experience circuit. Most of the time, the default narrative circuit is active, which is in charge of thinking about the past and the future and imagining stories and interpretations to help make sense of the world. For example, if a person catches a whiff of apple pie while he's walking down the street, he might recall a childhood memory of eating freshly baked pie at his grandmother's house. Then he remembers: *I should call Grandma to wish her a happy birthday. Oh, and I need to buy her a birthday present! And while I'm shopping for her gift, I should probably grab something for dinner*... and so on. In contrast, if that same person tries to be mindful as he walks down that street, his mind will activate its direct experience circuit. Instead of daydreaming about Grandma's house and creating a to-do list, he'll notice the notes of cinnamon in the aroma of the apple pie, the crunch of the pavement under his feet, and the chirping of birds as they flit from tree to tree.

Mindfulness training provides more awareness and control over these two circuits. In that University of Toronto study, the people who underwent eight weeks of intense mindfulness training could more easily recognize whether their minds were in narrative mode or direct experience mode, and they were better at consciously switching between the two than people who hadn't undergone mindfulness training. Those who hadn't practiced mindfulness would more often return to narrative mode without realizing it.

Mindfulness training makes people more aware of how they're experiencing the world and helps them become more active participants in their lives.

There's nothing wrong with being in narrative mode, but when it's active too often, people miss out on the fullness of life, and they forget that each present moment is a gift—an opportunity to experience the world more completely. Here's how to help a wandering mind and keep that direct experience mode turned on:

- **Be kind to yourself**: When thoughts start drifting—and again, they will; it's normal—bring back focus with compassion, just as someone would gently lead a wandering puppy back to its owner. Whenever the mind wanders, consider this an opportunity to retrain your focus.
- **Label thoughts**: Acknowledging thoughts for what they are—worrying, planning, daydreaming—can bring the mind back into direct experience mode and, over time, keep the mind from spending too much time immersed in narrative mode.
- **Visualize**: Imagine thoughts as items passing by on a conveyor belt, as glitter settling in a snow globe, or as waves in the ocean—when thoughts are racing, the sea will be rough, but in time, the water grows still.
- **Write**: When thoughts won't settle, try writing them in a journal or scribbling them on a Post-it note. Sometimes, they just need to be expressed on the page—to exist somewhere other than the mind.
- **Try *"Just this":*** Mindfulness instructor Laurie J. Cameron suggests repeating these words when

> focus starts to wander. When focus wanders, she says, tell yourself, "Just this email. Just this conversation. Just this book."

Remember that it's OK to daydream sometimes. It's neither possible nor healthy to maintain constant undivided attention, and these exercises aren't about controlling or restricting your thoughts. But learning how to intentionally settle your mind can help you calm down and focus whenever you feel anxious, scattered, or distracted.

CHAPTER THREE

# FACING LIFE'S CHALLENGES MINDFULLY

Being mindful won't solve every situation—but it can make these situations easier to cope with. Keep in mind that some techniques, like mindful breathing and checking in with the body's sensations, show up frequently in conversations about mindfulness because these strategies are helpful in many stressful situations. No matter where you are, you can use your body and breath to calm your emotions and focus your mind.

## TACKLING TESTS

It's completely normal to be nervous before tests; most people are! But here's how to approach them mindfully:

- **Study smart**: Start studying as early as possible, preferably at least a few days before the test. It can be overwhelming to review all the material at once, so try breaking it up into sections. While it's important to cover topics fully, try to focus on just one piece at a time.

- **Pause. Breathe**: If panic sets in during the test, take a moment to set down that pencil. Take a few slow, deep breaths, close your eyes, and focus on the sounds in the room and the feel of those breaths before returning to the task at hand. It may also help to take a few deep breaths every couple of pages.
- **Just one test for just one class**: In the heat of the moment, it's easy to forget that most tests aren't such a big deal in the grand scheme of life. The biology test that feels overwhelmingly huge right now will likely be a distant memory in five years' time. Yes, tests are important, and you need to try your best, but don't let your mind exaggerate the situation. If anxiety starts to spiral out of control, think, "This is just one test for just one class for just one year of school." And yes, this statement may not apply for a major test; but as with any test, just study hard, give it your all, and remember that your score doesn't define who you are. It can't capture the scope of your talents or any of the countless qualities that make you awesomely unique—qualities that couldn't possibly be measured by a bunch of academic questions on a sheet of paper or computer screen. So remember that these tests are limited in their power over you.

## CONQUERING PRESENTATIONS

Afraid of public speaking? You aren't alone. Even the most confident speakers are often nervous, and that

If you struggle with text anxiety, you're in good company. But mindfulness strategies can improve your study habits and help you relax when test day arrives.

anxiety may never disappear completely, but the following tips may help:

- **Practice, practice, practice:** Practice your presentation to anyone who will listen, whether that's a friend, a parent, or the family dog. Some people even find it helpful to practice their presentation in front of a mirror. Even just running through it once beforehand can be a huge confidence booster.
- **Cue yourself:** Write little reminders at the tops of flashcards or presentation notes. Just one word or a phrase, like "breathe" or "slow down," can

serve as a mindfulness cue to ease that feeling of rushed panic that sometimes takes over during times of stress. Don't forget to take advantage of natural pauses between presentation slides or sections—these are great opportunities to take a slow, deep breath before continuing.

- **Find your feet:** During shaky, panicked moments, feel your breath flowing all the way down to your feet, says psychologist and mindfulness instructor Christopher Willard. Just for a moment, focus all your awareness on your feet. Feel the weight in that spot, the sensations in your toes, the feeling of your socks and shoes up against your skin. What does the floor feel like? Press your weight down through your toes, imagining your breath grounding you to the spot and anchoring your emotions.
- **Remember:** People are often their own worst critics. If self-critical thoughts arise during a presentation, keep in mind that they don't necessarily reflect reality. Mistakes usually seem like a much bigger deal to the presenter than to the listeners. Know that it's OK to misspeak, stutter, or stumble over words; just take a deep breath, slow down, and try again.

## FALLING ASLEEP

Smartphone screens, computers, and TVs can all make falling asleep tricky, so consider winding down with an activity like reading or drawing. If you still have trouble sleeping, try one of the following techniques:

- **Take slow, deep breaths:** Slow breathing reminds the body that it's time to relax. One option is to try just focusing on breathing mindfully, paying attention to the sound of each inhale and exhale and noticing the natural rise and fall of the stomach with each breath. Alternatively, count the length of each inhale and exhale. Dr. Andrew Weil recommends the 4-7-8 technique: inhale through the nose for four seconds, hold it for seven, and exhale forcefully through the mouth for eight. It's fine to tweak these numbers according to what seems most comfortable, but try to keep the same 4-7-8 ratio (short inhaling, followed by a longer period of breath holding and exhaling) to maintain a slow, deliberate rhythm. This technique can be useful for relaxing in many stressful situations.
- **Don't check the time:** Yes, it's hard—but try to resist this temptation! Time checks will only create more panic and restlessness.
- **Use a relaxation exercise**: Try the body-scan exercise, paying attention to your breath and sensations and progressively relaxing each body part. Or, starting with the feet, imagine that each body part is very heavy; feel both feet and both legs sinking into the mattress, and imagine this heavy feeling slowly moving up the rest of the body until you feel complete-

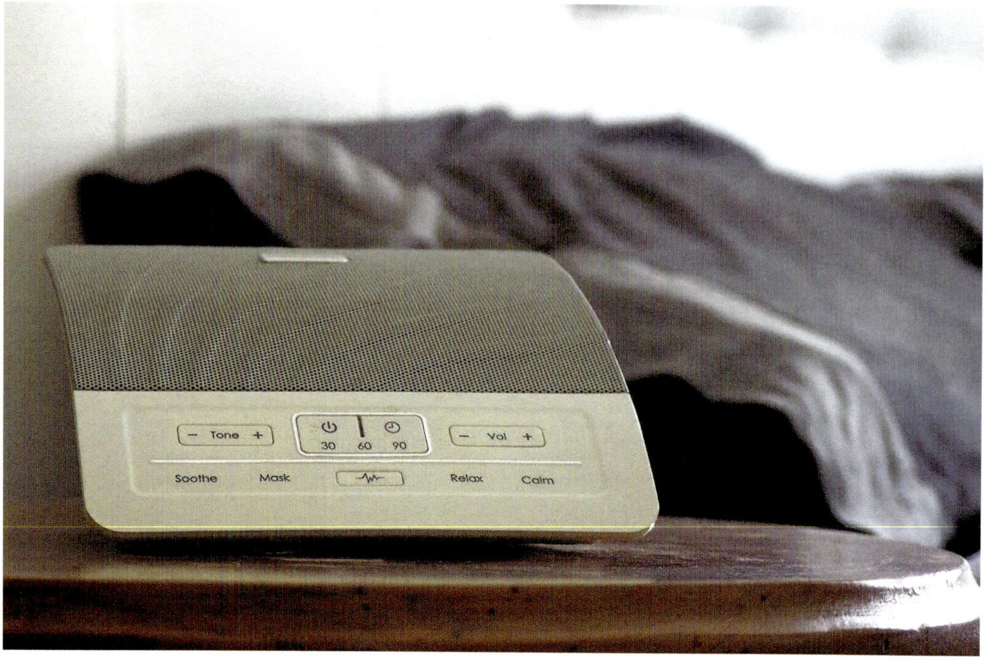


Most mindfulness techniques involve tuning in, but sometimes it's a good idea to tune *out.* White-noise machines like the one pictured here can help mask sounds that interfere with sleep.

ly relaxed. On cold nights, an actual heavy blanket can be used to create this effect as well.

- **Listen to relaxing sounds:** White-noise machines can help mask the sounds of whizzing cars or noisy neighbors. Or search for YouTube videos that contain sounds for sleep and relaxation.

## INTERACTING WITH OTHERS

Mindfulness can improve not only your relationship with yourself, but also your relationships with others. When

## BRINGING MINDFULNESS TO MELODIES AND CANVASES

For many people, music and art act as a gateway for a calmer, more focused mind. Here's how to bring mindfulness to whichever creative activities you enjoy:

- Listen mindfully: Listen to a song several times, and first, pay close attention to the lyrics and what they might mean. Then focus on individual instruments and voices; try to pick out a drum beat, for example, or tune in to a background singer's part. On each listen, try shifting your focus to something new, and see how that changes your experience of the music or your perception of the song.
- Play mindfully: Rather than relying on muscle memory, musicians can play their instruments mindfully by focusing on each finger movement. Remember that every note serves a purpose; instead of playing the piece on "autopilot," try to capture its emotion. Tell its story.
- Create mindfully: When painting, drawing, coloring, or working on some other artistic project, pay attention to the sensations involved, like the sound of the pencil strokes and the feel of the paintbrush as it slides across the canvas. Don't worry about what color to choose next or make judgments about the art itself. Just be present in the moment, and know that whatever you create is uniquely your own.

*(continued on the next page)*

*(continued from the previous page)*

Many people find that they are naturally more mindful when they're painting or drawing. An artistic hobby is a great way to relieve stress and practice living in the moment.

you make an effort to mindfully communicate with those around you, you open yourself up to more meaningful, more relaxed interactions. You can try these tips for any kind of social situation—discussions with friends and family, conversations with classmates and teachers, dates, and everything in between.

- **Listen—for real:** Sometimes you hear people speak without truly listening to them. Maybe you're planning your response when others are speaking, or you're simply waiting for someone

Teens can interact mindfully by listening carefully, replying thoughtfully, and tuning in to both their own and other people's feelings.

to pause or finish so you can have a turn. Listening wholeheartedly takes practice, but it speaks volumes. It says, *I respect you. You deserve my full attention.* As a bonus, mindful listening removes some of the pressure of social situations. Instead of having to divide your attention between someone else's words and what you want to say next, you need only to listen.

- **Reply thoughtfully:** When it's your turn in a conversation, don't feel rushed to get the words out. If needed, pause for a few moments to focus your thoughts.
- **Check in with your body:** Acknowledge the sensations in your body during this conversation, especially if it's a stressful or intense exchange. If your body is telling you that it's overwhelmed, take a few moments to focus on breathing slowly and deeply. Don't be afraid to say, "I need a break."
- **Notice other people's body language:** In addition to their words, try to pay attention to how people are speaking. What's their tone of voice like? Do they

sound worried, enthusiastic, calm? What do their movements and eye contact say about how they might be feeling? Noticing these details can help you become a more compassionate listener.

## PERFORMING ON THE FIELD AND IN THE CONCERT HALL

Practice is important, of course, but also consider using these techniques to prepare for athletic and musical performances:

- **Visualize:** Picture the performance going smoothly, and conjure up this image whenever those jittery feelings arise. Try to make the imagery as vivid as possible. What does the crowd sound like? How do your muscles feel as you prepare to make that kick? Can you "see" that soccer field?
- **Remember:** Panicked thoughts are just thoughts; they aren't necessarily the truth. It's OK to have self-critical thoughts, but don't hold on to them. Acknowledge them—"There's worry"—and allow them to pass. And if you make a mistake during the performance, that's fine, too. Notice it, then let it go. What happened in the past is in the past.
- **Breathe:** Take slow, deep breaths before the performance. Imagine exhaling tension and inhaling calm feelings. If some anxious feelings remain, embrace them. The ideal mindset for a performance is one of restful alertness: being focused and ready

to react without being relaxed to the point of sleepiness.

## COPING WITH CHRONIC PAIN AND MEDICAL PROCEDURES

Mindfulness can even help you deal with physical pain. Please know that this section is not at all suggesting that your pain is your fault. It's not—and it won't just disappear with a change in mindset—but mindfulness could help you cope.

If you experience chronic pain, for example, try to turn toward that pain with friendliness and curiosity instead of trying to resist it. Yes, that might sound crazy at first, but your instinctual attempts to solve, judge, or flinch away from this suffering only cause more frustration because you can't make the pain disappear with your thoughts. But you can work on changing your relationship to it. Let go of trying to fix the situation and just try to coexist with it, observe it, and approach it with curiosity.

Keep in mind that if this strategy ever feels like too much—if the pain is too intense or uncomfortable, and turning toward it doesn't feel like it's helping—it's OK to stop. In moments like these, shift your focus toward something else, like your breath, a nonpainful sensation in a different area of the body, or an outside distraction, like music, a TV show, or a book.

Focused distraction often works well during medical procedures, too. Instead of paying attention to what the health care professionals are doing, gently lead your mind to another sensation, such as the following:

Mindfully focusing on music and other distractions can be a powerful coping strategy in the face of chronic pain.

- **Sight:** Scroll through phone photos and try to pick out new details in them; focus on a poster or painting on the wall; or load up a game or puzzle to play.
- **Sound:** Listen to music, zeroing in on the song's lyrics or a specific instrument; or play the audiobook version of a favorite story.
- **Taste:** Focus on the flavor or texture of a piece of hard candy or mint.
- **Touch:** Tune into other areas of the body, tensing each part as much as possible and then relaxing it. Take slow, deep breaths, imagining nervousness leaving the body with each exhale and calmness entering with each inhale.

You can even try combining more than one sensation, especially during longer procedures or if you're nervous in the waiting room. Focus on the flavor of a candy and the words of an audiobook, for example, and challenge yourself to pay equal attention to both.

CHAPTER FOUR

# CREATING HABITS FOR A MINDFUL LIFE

Mindfulness is a superpower that everyone can access, and the more you exercise this power, the stronger and more natural it becomes. Every attempt to gently refocus a wandering mind is like a runner's lap, a pianist's scale, a figure skater's jump: with each repetition, it becomes easier.

But mindfulness is more than just a skill. It's a way of life. Instead of letting the world slip by unnoticed, people who practice mindfulness make the choice to live more fully and more comfortably. No matter what challenges they may be going through, mindful people know that they have valuable tools to help them cope, and they know that their thoughts do not have to control them.

Moving forward, it's important to establish a mindfulness routine because in the busyness of life, it's all too easy to slip back into old thought patterns. Turn mindfulness into a daily habit by checking in with your body and your emotions throughout the day. Tune into your surroundings on the walk to school or class; notice your breath before starting a test; and savor the joy

You can turn mindfulness into a lifelong habit by making an effort to be mindful during everyday activities, such as completing household chores or cuddling a pet.

that comes from hugging a friend, cuddling the cat, or listening to your favorite music.

## MINDFUL HABITS FOR PRODUCTIVITY

Most teens have had the experience of settling down to do some work, only to realize that four hours, three snacks, and two side conversations later, they've accomplished a whole lot of nothing. It's a frustrating situation because it comes with all the guilt of being unproductive without the satisfaction of completely relaxing. Unfortunately, there's no cure for procrastination or unproductivity—but mindfulness can help.

- **Work hard, play hard:** To work and relax more intentionally, try setting a timer (or download a productivity app that carries out this function, like Pomodoro). After twenty-five minutes of focused, productive work, take a five-minute, guilt-free break before resuming for another twenty-five minutes. After several productive sessions, take a longer break. Wholeheartedly enjoy this break—you've earned it.
- **Singletask:** Humans think they're great multitaskers, but science begs to differ. In a 2010 study published in *Psychonomic Bulletin & Review*, University of Utah researchers Jason Watson and David Strayer found that more than 97 percent of people cannot successfully complete more than one task at a time ... and if you think you're one of the exceptions, you aren't. According to their 2013 follow-up survey of more than three hundred students (published in *PLOS ONE*), the more confident a person was about her multitasking abilities, the worse she was at multitasking. The moral of this story? Make a to-do list, and concentrate on one item at a time. Life will feel less overwhelming, you'll make fewer mistakes, and you'll be more efficient.
- **Discover the magic of the Do Not Disturb phone setting:** Most smartphones have a Do Not Disturb mode; when this setting is activated, calls and texts

Scientific studies have shown that people are not good multitaskers. When tackling a to-do list, it's best to focus on one thing at a time.

come through silently, and only alarms make noise. Take advantage of this feature. It's a fantastic way to enhance mindfulness by avoiding the constant distractions of a noisy, vibrating phone. Do Not Disturb can be turned on manually, activated for a specific period of time, or scheduled (for example, during sleeping hours each night).

## MINDFUL HABITS FOR THANKFULNESS AND KINDNESS

When challenges come along, uplift others and you will find that you, too, are uplifted. And when you spread kindness to others during times of happiness, your joy will multiply. Some people react reflexively with anger and fear; take it upon yourself to react reflexively with thankfulness and kindness.

- **Start a gratitude list:** Write down ten things you're grateful for every day. On the hard days,

## MINDFUL MUTTS AND "MEDITATING" MICE

Dogs are masters at living in the present. Scold Fido for raiding the trash and by the time he heads out for his afternoon walk, he'll have long forgotten his crime. Perhaps that's why some people turn their dog's bark or their cat's meow into a cue to help them develop their own mindful habits. They use these sounds as reminders to pause, breathe, and notice their surroundings, so "woof" becomes a gentle nudge to live in the moment.

Animals have helped with the scientific research of mindfulness, too! Scientists at the University of Oregon wanted to know why meditation is so relaxing—and they turned to mice for answers. According to human brain scans, people who meditate tend to have increased development in the anterior cingulate cortex (ACC), a brain area involved in controlling emotions. Meanwhile, meditation seems to trigger theta waves, which are slow electrical pulses in the brain that are active when people feel deeply relaxed. The scientists guessed that these slow theta waves caused that increased ACC development in meditators. To test this theory, they got their hands on some special mice whose brain cells switched on in response to light. When the scientists shined slow, theta-wave-like pulses of light at these mice, their brain cells turned on in the ACC, and the mice acted calmer—almost as if they were meditating.

These results suggest that theta waves are powerful: they're probably one reason why mindfulness meditation is so relaxing, and by activating the ACC, they help create changes in the brain.

it might be difficult to think of ten reasons to be thankful, but do it anyway: the hard days are the days when you'll need this list the most. Feel free to include the big things ("I have food to eat"; "I have a roof over my head"), the little things ("I found a lucky penny"; "I saw a meme that made me laugh today"), and everything in between. There are no rules for gratitude lists; just pause, notice—and there are always reasons to smile, no matter how small—and write. It's an awesome mood booster. Consider keeping the lists in a journal or a folder (or even in the Notes section of your phone) because they're great to look back on during moments of adversity.

- **Send a gratitude list:** Write a letter to a friend or family member, and include a list of reasons why that person makes you smile, or send that person a list of your favorite memories together. It's a fantastic way to be mindful of meaningful relationships—and it'll make someone's day!
- **Practice self-compassion:** When self-critical thoughts arise, acknowledge them, and then ask yourself, "Would I say these things to somebody I care about?" If the answer is no, find the words you would say to that person, and say them to yourself.
- **Search for the good in others and tell them about it:** Do this even for the people who are difficult to get along with—especially for those people. Often, those who are challenging need compassion the most. Critical thoughts will arise

sometimes, but try to counter each judgment with something positive … and dig deep. Superficial compliments like, "He has a cool shirt," are nice, but they aren't nearly as meaningful as, "He is so generous," or even, "He tells the best jokes." It may not always be the right time to share these compliments, but whenever it seems appropriate, let people know. This small act of kindness might be just what they needed in that moment, and it could inspire them to become more mindful and compassionate toward others, too.

## YOU ARE WORTHY. YOU ARE CAPABLE.

*and i said to my body. softly. "i want to be your friend." it took a long breath. and replied, "i have been waiting my whole life for this."*
—Nayyirah Waheed

Mindfulness captures the essence of the poet Waheed's words (from an August 1, 2018 tweet); it's about befriending your body and mind and honoring physical and emotional feelings by giving them space to exist. It's about noticing the gifts we have been given and the gifts we have to offer. And it's about acknowledging our inner strength and learning how to use this strength to cope with challenges.

Ultimately, we are bigger than our experiences and bigger than the thoughts that fill our heads. Mindfulness gives you permission to embrace difficulties—not to

No matter what challenges you face throughout life, mindfulness techniques can help you stay focused, centered, and calm.

resist them, but to learn from them, and to allow them to shape you, but not to control you.

Remember that you carry mindfulness wherever you go; its power is always available to you. In times of trouble, turn to your breath, and remember: You matter, and you are enough. Life can be challenging, but you can do hard things. You've got this.

# 10 GREAT QUESTIONS TO ASK A THERAPIST ABOUT MINDFULNESS

1. Are you familiar with mindfulness training?
2. Is this the right time for me to work on mindfulness techniques?
3. Do you recommend I try mindfulness instead of medication or in addition to it?
4. Do you know of any local mindfulness groups or classes for teenagers or young adults?
5. Knowing my struggles, can you recommend specific mindfulness exercises that would be especially helpful?
6. Can you help me set a mindfulness routine that will work with my schedule?
7. In addition to mindfulness, what other coping strategies would you recommend for me?
8. Do you have any recommendations for mindfulness apps or videos?
9. If I'm feeling overwhelmed and I need more help to get through a difficult situation, which people or resources can I turn to?
10. How can I expect mindfulness to help with my specific difficulties?

# GLOSSARY

**adversity** Difficulty; a life challenge.

**amygdala** An area of the brain involved in detecting threats and processing fear.

**anterior cingulate cortex (ACC)** An area of the brain involved in controlling attention and emotion; similar to the prefrontal cortex.

**arachnophobic** Having an intense fear of spiders.

**body scan** A mindfulness exercise that involves paying attention to breathing and focusing on the sensations in one body part at a time.

**chronic** Long lasting.

**cue** A reminder to do something.

**direct experience circuit** A network in the brain that switches on when a person is being mindful.

**dwindling** Gradually decreasing.

**gratitude** A feeling of appreciation or thankfulness.

**insula** An area of the brain responsible for awareness and emotional processing.

**meditation** The act of focusing the mind.

**mindfulness** A state of mind that involves purposefully focusing attention on the present moment without judging or interpreting thoughts and experiences.

**narrative circuit (a.k.a. default circuit)** A network in the brain that switches on when a person is not being mindful.

**preconception** An assumption or old idea.

**prefrontal cortex** An area of the brain involved in controlling attention and emotion.

**quantify** To measure the size or amount of something.

**relapse** To experience symptoms of an illness again after a period of improvement.

**standardized** Having the same basic qualities. Experimental studies are often standardized so they can be fairly compared to each other.

**superficial** On the surface; often related to outward appearances instead of deeper qualities.

**suppress** To try not to think about something.

**theta wave** A slow, electrical pulse in the brain that is active when people feel deeply relaxed.

# FOR MORE INFORMATION

AnxietyBC Youth
311–409 Granville Street
Vancouver, BC V6C 1T2
Canada
(800) 668-6868
Website: http://youth.anxietybc.com
Facebook and Twitter: @AnxietyBC
AnxietyBC's goal is to raise awareness of anxiety disorders and provide resources to help people with anxiety. Their helpline provides free, confidential, anonymous help from a professional counselor twenty-four hours a day.

Centre for Mindfulness Studies
180 Sudbury Street, Unit C2
Toronto, ON M6J 0A8
Canada
(647) 524-6216
Website: https://www.mindfulnessstudies.com
Facebook and Instagram: @mindfulnessstudies
Twitter: @MindfulStudies
The Centre for Mindfulness Studies provides mindfulness training to the general public, health care workers, and other professionals.

Foundation for a Mindful Society
1776 I Street NW 9th Floor
Washington, DC 20006
Website: https://www.mindful.org

Facebook: @mindfulorg
Instagram: @mindfulmagazine
Twitter: @MindfulOnline
The Foundation for a Mindful Society is dedicated to promoting projects that accurately communicate the benefits of mindfulness to the public. It works toward its goal of a more mindful society through media outlets, including *Mindful* magazine, as well as through community activities such as conferences, meetings, and consulting.

Inward Bound Mindfulness Education (iBme)
PO Box 516
Concord, MA 01742
(978) 254-7082
Website: https://ibme.info
Email: contact@iBme.info
Facebook: @inwardboundmind
Instagram: @ibmeretreats
Twitter: @InwardBoundMind
iBme is a nonprofit organization that offers mindfulness retreats for teens and young adults. Through these retreats, participants learn mindfulness techniques, connect with peers and mentors in small groups, and engage in a variety of workshop activities.

Mind & Life Institute
210 Ridge McIntire Road, Suite 325
Charlottesville, VA 22903
(434) 338-7380
Website: https://www.mindandlife.org

Email: info@mindandlife.org
Facebook and Twitter: @mindandlife
Instagram: @mindandlifeinstitute
The Mind and Life Institute is devoted to examining the overlap between science and Buddhist traditions such as meditation.

National Center for Complementary and Integrative Health (NCCIH)
9000 Rockville Pike
Bethesda, MD 20892
(888) 644-6226
Website: https://nccih.nih.gov
Email: info@nccih.nih.gov
Facebook: @nih.nccih
Instagram: @nih_nccih
Twitter: @NIH_NCCIH
NCCIH is a governmental agency that promotes scientific research related to complementary and integrative medicine and health, including mindfulness meditation.

Tools for Peace (TFP)
75 S. Grand, Suite 217
Pasadena, CA 91105
(626) 564-0700
Website: http://www.toolsforpeace.org
Email: info@toolsforpeace.org
Facebook, Twitter, and Instagram: @toolsforpeace
Tools for Peace is devoted to bringing mindfulness training to people of every socioeconomic background, especially youth.

# FOR FURTHER READING


Burdick, Debra, and Lara Webb. *Mindfulness for Teens with ADHD: A Skill-Building Workbook to Help You Focus and Succeed*. Oakland, CA: Instant Help Books, 2017.

Davenport, Barrie, and S. J. Scott. *The Mindfulness Journal: Daily Practices, Writing Prompts, and Reflections for Living in the Present Moment*. Self-published, 2017.

Landau, Jennifer, ed. *Teens Talk About Anxiety and Depression*. New York, NY: Rosen Publishing, 2018.

Mindfulness Project, The. *I Am Here Now: A Creative Mindfulness Guide and Journal*. TarcherPerigee, 2016.

Patel, Meera Lee. *Start Where You Are: A Journal for Self-Exploration*. New York, NY: TarcherPerigee, 2015.

Porterfield, Jason. *Teen Stress and Anxiety*. New York, NY: Rosen Publishing, 2014.

Purcell, Mark C., and Jason R. Murphy. *Mindfulness for Teen Anger: A Workbook to Overcome Anger and Aggression Using MBSR and DBT Skills*. Oakland, CA: Instant Help Books, 2014.

Staley, Erin. *Defeating Stress and Anxiety*. New York, NY: Rosen Publishing, 2016.

Vo, Dzung X. *The Mindful Teen: Powerful Skills to Help You Handle Stress One Moment at a Time*. Oakland, CA: Instant Help Books, 2015.

Willard, Christopher. *Mindfulness for Teen Anxiety: A Workbook for Overcoming Anxiety at Home, at School, and Everywhere Else*. Oakland, CA: Instant Help Books, 2014.

# BIBLIOGRAPHY

BBC News. "Cave Rescue: How Did the Thai Boys Survive Underground?" July 11, 2018. https://www.bbc.com.

Cameron, Laurie J. *The Mindful Day: Practical Ways to Find Focus, Calm, and Joy From Morning to Evening*. Washington, DC: National Geographic, 2018.

Essex Meditation. "Testimonials." Celebrity Meditators. Retrieved August 19, 2018. http://www.essexmeditation.org.

Farb, Norman A. S., Zindel V. Segal, et al. "Attending to the Present: Mindfulness Meditation Reveals Distinct Neural Modes of Self-Reference." *Social Cognitive and Affective Neuroscience* 2, no. 4 (2007): 313–22.

Healthy Lifestyle Brands, LLC. "Video: Breathing Exercises: 4-7-8 Breath." Weil: Andrew Weil, M.D. Retrieved September 2, 2018. https://www.drweil.com.

Kabat-Zinn, Jon. *Wherever You Go, There You Are: Mindfulness Meditation in Everyday Life.* New York, NY: Hachette Books, 2010.

Konnikova, Maria. "Multitask Masters." *The New Yorker,* May 7, 2014. https://www.newyorker.com.

Kuyken, William, Fiona C. Warren, et al. 2016. "Efficacy of Mindfulness-Based Cognitive Therapy in Prevention of Depressive Relapse." *JAMA Psychiatry* 73, no. 6.

Obasi, Chidi N., Roger Brown, et al."Advantage of Meditation over Exercise in Reducing Cold and Flu Illness is Related to Improved Function and Quality of Life." *Influenza and Other Respiratory Viruses* 7, no. 6 (2013): 938–44.

Rosenkranz, Melissa A., Richard J. Davidson, et al. "A Comparison of Mindfulness-Based Stress Reduction and an Active control in Modulation of Neurogenic Inflammation." *Brain, Behavior, and Immunity* 27 (2012).

Rowling, J. K. *Harry Potter and the Prisoner of Azkaban*. New York, NY: Arthur A. Levine Books, 1999.

Tang, Yi-Yuan, Britta Holzel, and Michael Posner. "The Neuroscience of Mindfulness Meditation." *Nature Reviews Neuroscience* 16, no. 4 (2015).

Tsafou, Kalliopi-Eleni, Denise TD De Ridder, et al. "Mindfulness and Satisfaction in Physical Activity: A Cross-Sectional Study in the Dutch Population." *Journal of Health Psychology* 21, no. 9 (2016): 1817–27.

Waheed, Nayyirah (@nayyirahwaheed). 2018. "And i said to my body. softly. 'i want to be your friend.' it took a long breath. and replied 'i have been waiting my whole life for this.'" Twitter, August 1, 2018, 8:53 a.m. https://twitter.com.

Willard, Christopher. *Mindfulness for Teen Anxiety: A Workbook for Overcoming Anxiety at Home, at School, and Everywhere Else*. Oakland, CA: Instant Help Books, 2014.

Williams, Mark, and Danny Penman. *Mindfulness: An Eight-Week Plan for Finding Peace in a Frantic World*. Emmaus, PA: Rodale Books, 2012.

Wong, Sam. "'Meditating Mice' Reveal Secrets of Mindfulness Training." *New Scientist*, February 20, 2017.

# INDEX

## ABOUT THE AUTHOR

Kerry Elizabeth Benson received her undergraduate degree from Connecticut College, where she studied neuroscience, and one of her main areas of research was the psychology and neurobiology of stress. In 2018, she received a master's degree in science writing from Johns Hopkins University and is pursuing a career in that field.

## PHOTO CREDITS

Cover Zdenka Darula/Shutterstock.com; back cover Photo by marianna armata/Moment/Getty Images; p. 5 Kyodo News/Getty Images; p. 6 ESB Professional/Shutterstock.com; pp. 8, 19, 33, 45 Lina Bruins/EyeEm/Getty Images; p. 9 PictureLux/The Hollywood Archive/Alamy Stock Photo; p. 10 Joe Seer/Shutterstock.com; p. 14 The Boston Globe/Getty Images; p. 15 pixelheadphoto digitalskillet/Shutterstock.com; p. 20 siamionau pavel/Shutterstock.com; p. 23 Hugo Felix/Shutterstock.com; p. 25 Martin Novak/Moment/Getty Images; p. 27 M4OS Photos/Alamy Stock Photo; p. 30 Martin Barraud/Caiaimage/Getty Images; p. 35 Firma V/Shutterstock.com; p. 38 luca pbl/Shutterstock.com; p. 40 Lou Jones/Lonely Planet Images/Getty Images; p. 41 silverkblackstock/Shutterstock.com; p. 44 wong yu liang/Shutterstock.com; p. 46 Lapina/Shutterstock.com; p. 48 Monkey Business Images/Shutterstock.com; p. 52 stockphoto mania/Shutterstock.com.

Design: Michael Moy; Layout: Tahara Anderson;
Editor: Jennifer Landau; Photo Researcher: Sherri Jackson